In the Search for Love. A Book about Emotional Pain and Pleasure of Loving.

Laurent Asteria

Published by Laurent Asteria, 2024.

Table of Contents

In the Search for Love: The Book about Emotional Pain and Pleasure | of Loving. | By Laurent Asteria.................................1

Introduction. 3

When Your Husband Has Abnormally Big Penis and You Discover It after Marriage...6

Why Don't You Love Me?...9

This Is the Love All Men Desire. 12

My Girl Called Me a Thief When I Caught Her with a Boy in Her Room.. 23

I Have a Loving Heart. 27

Sources of Violence in Romantic relationships................... 39

The Confused Seducer.. 41

Everybody can be Loved. 43

Females Carry Beauty but Do not Own It............................. 45

Love and Social Disorders. 47

Sexual-social Crises in Romantic Relationships................... 49

Strength and Confidence as Important Qualities in Romantic Relationships. 51

The Use of Science and Art to Improve Romantic Relationship.... 53

Why Betrayals in Romantic Relationships is a Common Practice?... 55

There is Beauty in Everybody. 57

Why True Love is Hard to Find? 58

How to Deal with Infidelity or Betrayals in Romantic Relationships. 60

The Root cause of Crises in Romantic Relationships. 63

Effects of Dissatisfaction in Romantic Relationships........................ 65

Do You Have a Cruel Partner? Find it Why and How to Deal with Them.. 67

End. | References 69

In the Search for Love: The Book about Emotional Pain and Pleasure of Loving.

By Laurent Asteria.

Introduction.

This book is a collection of short stories based on real experiences people encounter during their love lives. It includes both the bitter and sweets faced when people plunge into the pool of loving, which I think they should be imparted to interested individuals, experienced couples or the amateurs. It is my greatest desire that this work becomes a triumph to those distresses love brings us, as well as a steer towards true enjoyment that we have been yearning from love.

Currently, many societies in the World face an increase in violence and social crises caused by romantic and sexual dissatisfactions. Badly enough, these crises can spread their effects to other aspects of life such as economy, social relations, health *et cetera*.

Reports about violence in romantic relationships have been published frequently in media; one of the reasons which are commonly mentioned is romantic jealousy. These incidences can discourage people to embark into courtship and/or marriages, and eventually weaken welfare of families and societies in general.

Due to the importance of marriage in family and social welfare, there is a strong need for human beings to remind each other about this importance in order to protect the value of romantic relationships, or marriages. We need to share our knowledge, skills and experience which will enable us improve our understanding on how to keep romantic relationship among couples and avoid the risk of being victims of romantic jealousy.

In this book, the author presents to you the knowledge and skills written by psychologists, philosophers and researchers of romantic relationships and marriages from different parts of the word, of past centuries and current. This book will guide you to seek for a solution to prevalence of violence caused by romantic jealousy, lack of true love, infidelity, and eventually to build strong relationships among couples.

Authors David Rosenhan and Martin Seligman in their book titled *Abnormal Psychology*, published in 1995, page 472, give a statement which tends to imply that dissatisfaction in romantic relationships can cause a combination of symptoms in people, some of which are not related to sex. Examples of these symptoms are morbidity, perversion, and others.

Authors Linda Meeks and Philip Heit, in their book called *Sexuality and Character Education*, published in 2001, page 49, write that, some people feel sexual excitement when they hurt others. In psychology, this behavior which is a problem is called *sadism*.

Two ancient Greek philosophers; Socrates and Plato had similar views about evils. Both of them believed that ignorance is the root of all evils (Pecorino, 2001; Pigliucci, 2011). This belief is still relevant even in crises which occur in modern romantic relationships. Nowadays, most of crises which occur in romantic relationships are initiated or intensified by failure of couples to understand why one partner acts or speaks something.

Sometimes it happens in romantic relationships that one partner acts or speaks something for good reason; but it is wrongly interpreted by their lover; if the lover (the wrong interpreter) is not ready to ignore or comply humbly to the acts or remarks, they may want to revenge; but actually the revenge is only due to wrong interpretation.

Professor Richard A. Carroll, a behavioral psychologist and psychiatrist, from Northwestern University, Chicago-USA, is quoted by an online magazine, *The Frontier Medicine Institute* saying that "asking why people have sex is akin to asking why people eat". This statement implies that romantic relationship can be compared with food due to the importance of both in the propagation of species.

All these quotations show how the field of sex has been under study by various professionals, particularly psychologists and philosophers. So I argue you to read this book thoroughly, get along with me in these writings as I am going to mould you in the way you would have prayed the God to.

When Your Husband Has Abnormally Big Penis and You Discover It after Marriage.

It was a Saturday evening when one of our friends took us to the beach for recreation. I sat with my two friends in one of circular huts built with dry coconut leaves along the beach shore. On a table, there were glasses half full of liquors and bottles of a variety of beverages and liquors, we regularly took sips of the liquids and engaged in casual conversations.

The beach was busy as a custom for weekends; different people moved here and there singly, in pairs and in groups; while others dived and swam in the ocean water. Along the shore, few meters from the shore line, there were cafes and equipments set for children's plays. While children played blissfully in their arranged places, other people sat inside the cafes and the huts to take beach snacks and drinks.

Ocean breeze blew gently through the beach atmosphere and spread the beautiful aroma of a variety of cuisines that were cooked in the cafes. There were a variety of entertainments including that of dancers who exhibited their performances on a platform in front of an open ground. All these, and the beach view, made this area extremely pleasant.

As we went on with our casual conversations and taking drinks, two girls moved our way, they came to the shore to take a break after some times of swimming. Both of them wore beach clothes; G strings under their bikini briefs and they covered their breasts with scanty brassiere.

"No, it's too big, I can't tolerate him anymore. I don't even enjoy the sex!" I heard one of the girls complaining earnestly to her friend when they were close to us, I couldn't quickly understand the origin of their conversation because I caught it in its midway; it looked like the conversation began when they were in water.

Fortunately, I happened to know the girl; her complaints intrigued my interest to listen to the full story of her circumstances. Although she discontinued the conversation when they reached our table, I whispered to her and requested if she was willing to reveal the full story to me. Thank God that she never hesitated to give me her cooperation; therefore we held a private conversation in low voice, between the two of us.

Although I don't support her inclination to disclose the situation of her husband such easily, I am thankful for the opportunity which enabled me acquire the information which I use positively for the wellbeing of others, provided that I render the girl and her husband anonymous.

With some tinge of shyness and reluctance, she told me about the big size of the penis of her husband, which causes annoyance to her when they make love. She was a girl who had just been married to her husband; she never had slept with him before their marriage as she was trying to adhere to religious and social ethics in which she was raised.

After getting into the marriage, then she found herself caught up into the mess. Badly enough, she didn't know where to bring her complaints for help because she thought the matter was somehow embarrassing. Also she couldn't run away from the marriage because they had made a formal wedding, they didn't just pick up each other from the streets. Furthermore, her husband had already paid a huge amount of money as a bride price, and her parents had already spent the money which was difficult for them to return it.

Now the girl was in a dilemma, not knowing what to do. I quickly tried to ponder about what I should advise her, but there was no quick idea coming to my mind by that time. But what I quickly discerned is the fact that, her marriage was about to enter into a marital crisis. Here, my mind gets stressed with some questions about the marital crisis which would arise in their marriage. First, who was to be blamed for the crisis in case it occurred? Is it the husband for his big penis, or the wife for not discovering the matter earlier? What do you think would have been done before to avoid the crisis?

The girl and her husband had tried hard to adhere to the social and religious ethics; that is why they refrained from engaging in sex before marriage; how could this ethical principle of refraining from premarital sex help them to escape from the marital crisis? I would like to pose this question to the readers of this story: Do you personally adhere to this ethical principle of abstaining from premarital sex? Don't you think there is a need to review this ethical principle so that to rescue other future couples so that they don't fall into the same predicament?

Let me put the question in this way: What do you think, should couples be allowed by ethics to engage in premarital sex so that they understand their future spouses prior to getting into marriage in order to avoid the envisaged future crisis as I have shown above?

Why Don't You Love Me?

I use to sell snacks in a canteen at a secondary school where I have fallen in love to a girl student known as Khadiyah. Today after I finish selling snacks, I remain at school waiting to see the girl when she leaves the school at thirty past two in the afternoon. In the afternoon students are allowed to return home. I see Khadiyah walks with her two friends past a tree under which I stand; their school bags hang from their shoulders.

I am strongly pleased seeing Khadiyah very close to me, and catch a sweet fragrance of her perfume. And when she walks away I feel pain, "Why she hasn't even greeted me?" I grieve inwardly at a perception of being disdained. Stupidly, I am tempted to follow her behind.

When they have left a school compound, I see three boys surround Khadiyah and bully her. I say from the back, "Hey, leave her alone!" I point a warning finger to the boys. I move to the boys as they ignore my warning, and harass the girl while her friends stay away in fear of the boys. When I reach them, I find myself in their fierce hands; they beat me heavily so that I lose my conscious. Passers-by stand few meters away, only watching while I am beaten. Then the boys run away leaving me lying alone on the ground.

When I get back to my consciousness, I realize I am in a health center where I am admitted with my body wounded, I see a nurse and my two relatives beside my bed. "Sorry my brother, you will be okay." Mkude, my young brother comforts me in a gloomy voice.

"Where am I?" I ask as I wrinkle my face in pain.

"You are in a dispensary; you were brought here by people who found you lying on a ground after you were beaten." The nurse tells me.

I try to retrieve events which happened earlier before I lost conscious, "Oh, what about Khadiyah? Is she okay? Where is she now?" I ask gloomily after I remember the incident.

"Who is Khadiyah?" The nurse asks my brother.

"For now let us focus on your wellbeing, don't worry about others." Mkude tells me, a little bit annoyed. I ask them about Khadiyah not caring whether they know her or not.

"I am afraid I am not going to recover if I don't see her, can you please help me see her even for a while?" I insist anxiously. All people here exchange glances as they are unable to understand me.

"Who is Khadiyah?" The nurse asks again.

"We don't know her." My relatives reply. Then silence takes over for a while. I use this time to think of how ridiculous I am for showing strong interest for the girl who doesn't even know me.

"Can you tell us a little about the girl you are talking about? We have no idea of her." Mkude asks me as he wraps his arms around his chest. I try to think how I should explain her to them, but what bothers me is the uncertainty of how I will be construed if I mention the girl, owing to the fact that she is too young to me, and she doesn't even know me.

"It's that girl in the street next to ours, she studies at Mshikamano secondary school." I say.

It is not hard for my brothers to recognize the girl when they hear the details, "Aha that girl, now I know her. But why so concerned about her, is she your friend?" Mkude asks me.

I mention her to be the reason for me being here, that I was assaulted by boys when I was trying to rescue the girl from the boys who were disturbing her. "So far I don't know her circumstances." I mourn.

I ask my relatives to check Khadiyah at their home, and if they find her ask the girl come to see me in the dispensary. I feel she is the only way I will recover. This request seems somewhat crazy to my brothers, they remain quiet for a while to swallow the request and see how they are going to deal with it.

Later in the evening, I get visitors in my ward. It's my mother, my brother Mkude, a young girl and another woman. I happen to know them all, and for sure, when I see them my heart glows with happiness. I rise from the bed and sit upright with a wide smile.

"Welcome, here he is." My mother tells the visitors as they move closer to my bed.

With my eyes riveted to the girl, I unfold my right arm and hand it to her, to make a greeting. I see the girl offers her hand to me reluctantly; I grab her hand and hold it passionately with my both hands. Finally Khadiyah is here, but with an obvious surprise and apathy in her face.

"You said you want to see the girl, she is here now, what can she do for you?" My mother asks me when the visitors surround me on my bed. I remain silent groping a proper word to tell; still holding the girl's hand with mine.

"I, I just wanted to see her. I was wondering how she is doing." I finally say.

"Who is this man? I do not even know him. By the way, with all your sane mind you called me to come and talk to this ill!" Khadiyah grimaces as she says these words. She sniffs as if she is struggling to escape unpleasant smell, then she turns to the door and run away.

I try hard to accept the pain I feel when I see Khadiyah treats me like this. I thought at least she would be sympathetic for what had happened to me while I was trying to rescue her.

"Why don't you love me Khadiyah! Why don't you love me? For how long will I have to suffer this pain?" I cry as I lie clumsily on my bed.

This Is the Love All Men Desire.

I am seated just in front of a lady with an extremely delightful appearance; once I throw my eyes on her, I get an anguish which cajoles me to look at her more and more. My blood agitates with excitement as my eyes pass through her face and the height of her body. However, the lady seems nonchalant as she is engrossed in her business. I lie my back on a bed and stare at her with great enjoyment.

All these happen when I am in our bedroom with my wife who has just finished washing herself, and now she is taking care of her skin after the wash. As I look at her, I recall the troubles I suffered in those days when I was in search for her, I release a gentle sigh when I smile slightly and call her, "Stella,"

She turns to me with her usual meek expression when she talks to me, "Yes my husband," she says. Then I continue, "You know what," I pause and rise from the bed, step to her back and wrap my arms around her waist, "I feel sorry for you."

It looks like this statement shocks her, "Why?" She asks as she turns to me, surprised.

"I am afraid you don't deserve these miseries we experience in our life."

"Miseries?" She asks again, even more shocked, "What are you trying to say?"

I release a sigh again, settle my chin over her head and hold her tighter around my arms as if I tell her to relax. Then I say, "You are so cute and innocent that you only belong to comfortable life of which you have no access. What you deserve is love, enjoyment and relaxation." As I say this, she turns and looks at me, so our eyes meet. She makes a smile and hides her face on my chest.

"Do you think I am not comfortable? When I have you I feel I have all the comforts." She says in her innocent voice, and then she also wraps her arms around my neck so that our bodies press against each other. I want to pull away from her when I remember I should be going to farm but I hesitate, craving to continue enjoy her warm morning touch.

"You should be going to work now." She tells me as she caresses my chest with her right hand while her left arm still around the back of my neck. Reluctantly, I let her off my arms, but she grabs my right hand and pulls me to the sitting room.

In the sitting room, I sit on a table to take a breakfast; there is a thermos flask containing sorghum porridge and a plate of seethed sweet potatoes. My wife, Stella pours the sorghum porridge into a cup for me, "Welcome dear." She tells me as she opens the cover from the small basket containing the potatoes.

"Did you offer Asteria something for her lunch at school?" I ask when she lifts the cap; vapor exudes from the potatoes, implying they are just taken from fire.

"Yeah, I handed her three sweet potatoes. You know me well; I wouldn't let my daughter starve at school while she has a caring mother." My wife replies. Asteria is our nine years old daughter, now she is in primary school, standard five. She leaves for school early in the morning and returns at 15 hrs; therefore she uses to carry something with her to eat at school, to make her active with studies.

When I finish taking the breakfast, I take a hoe and machete and walk to farm. I leave my wife home preparing to open her business in which she works to plait women hair in payment. She runs the business at our home where women who need to plait their hair visit her and pay her money for their hair to be plaited.

On my way to the farm my mind is plagued with the thoughts about my wife, I feel myself among the luckiest people in the world for having a wife like her. The memories of her caring for me give me strength and courage to struggle in the farm for her, to search for wealth and all things she would need, I vow to do anything in my capability to satisfy her. I wish I had all the wealth of this World so that I gave them to her, I think she deserves all the wealth of this World.

At 18 hrs in the evening, I walk back home. I didn't have to return home for lunch in the afternoon because there is a plenty of foods in the farm, you just need to have a source of fire, or pick fruits from trees to get something to satiate an empty stomach.

At home, I am hugged by my wife Stella and my daughter Asteria who has returned from school. I hand over a basket packed with stuffs from farm to my wife who keeps it in the kitchen. I turn to Asteria, my daughter, "Oh girl, how was the school today?" I ask as I beckon her to follow me inside. I sit on a wooden chair, in the sitting room and tell her to show me her school work.

When I am satisfied with the work in my daughter's books, I go to my bedroom to take my towel so that I wash myself, my wife follows me. Inside the bedroom my wife sits on the bed, beside me. She cries as she tells me the news that happened in the afternoon when she was plaiting her customer.

"My husband, I am sorry for this but I have to tell it anyway." She speaks as she cries, leaning her head on my shoulder.

"What is it?" I ask quickly, a sudden thumping of my heart makes me breath uncontrollably.

"It's about Kimgidu," She says worriedly.

When I hear the name, I quickly try to recall any person in our neighborhood with this name, I only remember the famous rich man in our village, Kimgidu. But I wonder if this is a person my wife refers to, "Kimgidu who?" I ask to elicit more details from her.

"Don't you know Kimgidu, the prominent person in our village?" She reproaches politely.

"Enhe, what disaster happened to him?" I ask when I get ascertained it's this well known person in our village for his wealth. I presume the man must be in a trouble having seen my wife crying when she mention him.

"No. It's not like that." She falters. "I love you my husband." She says softly when she moves her face close to mine so that they bind together.

Her actions leave me still puzzled. "You know I am in confusion, can you please be straight. What is the matter, what is going on?" I say a little angrily.

Then my wife recounts the story, "At first I dismissed it but now I see it's becoming serious. When I was waiting for customers in the afternoon, there came a woman claiming to be sent by Kimgidu, she told me the thing she has been telling me for sometimes now."

"What is it?" I interrupt.

"She says Kimgidu loves me, and he is ready to give me anything if I accept being in liaison with him."

I recline my back on the bed, release a deep sigh and remain silent; to allow myself recover from the tense state. I spend a few second staring my wife who also looks at me boldly. "You say she has been telling you this thing for sometimes now; then why you didn't tell me?" I ask, slightly disappointed.

"As I have told you I dismissed it because I thought it would stop. I tell you because I see it prolong, I think now you should know it so that I hear your stance."

"Okay, thanks for being faithful and loving. You leave it to me and we shall see what to do." I tell her as I sit upright. I pull her close to me and pet her back, and then I stand up and go to the bathroom.

When I wash myself I ponder about what I should do to deal with the matter circumstance my wife has just told me. I think of running to Kimgidu's home and beat him to death but my intention shrinks at the contemplation of his wealthy and fame. "How am I going to execute this intention? All I am is nothing but bones and flesh sculptured in a form called human being, a poor villager." I contemplate desperately. I fight back a sensation of jealous and anticipated betrayal. I don't want to believe that my wife rejects all the cajoleries of the village's richest man just to live with me. I realize I am plagued with worry.

The worry does not let me settle, I visit my friend Lawi in an attempt to search for support and advice. At Lawi's home I get surprised seeing that he smiles when I tell him about this matter, "My friend, if you are intelligent enough, you and your wife are going to be rich. This is money!" He tells me, a beam of smile still lingers on his face.

I look at him with a daze, and when he realizes I have not understood him he continues, "You know this man is rich and famous, when you entrap him in a scandal of sleeping with another man's wife, he will be would easily surrender whatever you instruct him."

When I hear his remark I smile faintly, then a wide beam of smile spreads throughout my face. "And how am I going to do it?" I ask inquisitively.

He goes on, "It's like this, talk to your wife and arrange how you are going to execute it; your wife must consent to participate. Let her deceive him she has agreed to sleep with him, and then prepare a plan to record evidence like pictures which you will use to blackmail him. I am sure he will not deny offering a substantial amount of money in compensation."

"My friend, you want to put me in danger." I criticize him as I shake my head.

"Why?" Lawi asks.

"Do you think it is that simple? You speak as if you don't know Kimgidu." I say when I look to his face. I see he stays quiet for sometimes and scratches his chin with his right hand.

"May be you should team up with somebody else, especially his business rivals." He suggests.

"There you are; now I appreciate your wits." I am impressed with this suggestion, I laugh as I offer him a hand.

I am paranoid that Kimgidu won't stop until he has accomplished his wish for my wife, and what if my wife becomes reluctant? He may think of using force, right? I am determined to defend my marriage as there is nothing I love in this life like my wife. I see Kimgidu a threat to my marriage and even to the security of my family; therefore I vow to do anything possible to prevent this threat.

I quickly try to examine among the village tycoons, to get the best person I can use against Kimgidu. "Who do you think I should conspire with?" I ask Lawi after short moment of silence.

"Dudukudo." Lawi responds quickly as if he was waiting for the question.

"I know Dudukudo, he is a true rival of Kimgidu; but he is from a neighboring village. Do you think he is fit for this?" I become a bit skeptic.

My friend Lawi turns his face down and bits his lips, I let him alone to figure it out. Then he looks at me and says, "I think that is an advantage to us. If we use somebody out of our village it will easily exclude us as being involved in the plot. Let Kimgidu's capture look unplanned."

The next day I go with Lawi to Dudukudo's village. We inform him about the issue and thanks God he takes it as we expected. "It's good that you have decided to deal with him, I know the man very well. He has been doing this to other women several places, a lot of people talk negatively about him."

"If we will be able to get photos of him with your wife ready-handed on bed, that will be his end. I will promote he pays you huge compensation or otherwise further the issue for him be sued." Dudukudo tells us.

We ask him to give his idea of how we should execute this plot. "It depends with the nature of your wife, her readiness and wits. I think I need to talk to the lady before saying my plans." He suggests. We set another appointment tomorrow for him to meet my wife and then we leave.

The next day I bring my wife to meet Dudukudo at his home, Lawi escorts me. We sit at the fruit garden behind his house. Dudukudo talks to my wife to enquire her ability to handle Kimgidu. Today I see Dudukudo is more cordial and generous than yesterday, our conversation is accompanied with a variety of meals prepared for us by his servants.

"Now I am satisfied." He says when he has asked his tricky questions to try the ingenuity of my wife and her readiness to undertake the assignment against Kimgidu. "But," he poses and scribbles on the ground with a stick he is holding. He looks to my wife, then to me, "How long have you lived together?" He asks.

"Ten years." I reply, "I married my wife when she was still a young girl."

"Do you have children?"

"Yeah."

"How many?" He asks again.

"Only one." I reply. Although I am a bit surprised with his questions which sound more personal, I consider this question as his approach to design a better plan of dealing with Kimgidu.

"Okay." Finally he says, scratching the back of his neck while his eyes riveted to my wife. "For a lady like you I see the task will be so simple. I will give you my men to work with you; they will be having a camera. You should also have a cellular phone for communication, when Stella takes a room with that man the camera man must know and be around, off course he will be backed with other people who will pretend to be brothers of Stella and they accidentally apprehend their sister with another man in a room. I think this trick will eliminate possible suspicion that there was a conspiracy.

We agree in this plan, we also agree to give the participants some time to rehearse before going into the field. When we leave back home, Dudukudo furnish us with a variety of offerings; three domestic fowls and a bucket of fresh milk drawn from cattle he keeps at his compound, then he takes us home on his car.

As usual, I wake up early in the morning and walk to farm. While Asteria goes to school, my wife spends the first days rehearsing the task she has to carry out against Kimgidu, she meets with Dudukudo's men to familiarize each other and practice the task. In the evening, I return home and my wife shows me a bag brought by Dudukudo, "Dudukudo came to take me here in the morning and gave us this."

I kneel slightly and probe what is inside the bag; I see female garments and shoes. "Did you ask for this?" I ask my wife.

"No. Myself I was reluctant to accept it but he insisted to give." My wife replies.

"May be he wants to keep you attractive so that you can easily win that man." I presume and my wife nods, "I think so."

"Did you test them?" I ask again.

"No. I thought you should know first." I smile when I hear this answer. "By the way, how was the rehearsal?"

"I see it is simple, I think by tomorrow we will have mastered everything." She replies.

When I am in the farm next day my wife comes sweating and upset. She dresses nicely though, as if she belongs to an elite family, her hand holds something. I put the hoe down and watch her coming my way. She hugs me and cries, "What have I wronged the God!"

"What? Why?" I ask as I don't understand her.

"It's Dudukudo, he is just like Kimgidu." My wife tells me while crying.

I look at her then I look at the key she is holding. She goes on saying, "Dudukudo also wants me to betray you and sleep with him; he has offered me a car."

I wrinkle my face and press her tightly against me. We remain pressed like this for a considerable moment in which time I feel warm streams chafe down my cheeks. I feel like I am carrying the earth planet over my head, and for sure this feels heavy. I take my wife inside the hut we use to take rest when it is too sunny or rainy.

We sit inside and ask Stella to explain it to me in details. Now I see I get two enemies when I was trying to escape one. Why shouldn't I cry?

"Wait!" I say abruptly as I stand up.

"What do you want to do?" Stella asks me as she holds me back.

"What do they think of me; let me show them a bit who I am."

"No. Don't panic like that, it's simple. Provided that I love you, we can easily counter them." Stella tells me. Then she continues, "Since Kimgidu and Dudukudo are enemies to each other, then let me use this enmity against both of them."

When she pauses I stare her and say, "Go ahead."

"I will pretend to accept both of them and let them fight. When one is defeated, the other will easily be subjected to the legal actions."

I consider the idea for a while and ask, "Won't you fall into giving yourself to them?"

"No, I swear. No one will penetrate me even an inch!" She guarantees.

I hug my wife.

Kimgidu sends a phone message to his rival Dudukudo and argues fiercely with him as they are used to. This happens shortly after my wife Stella showed the readiness of getting into a liaison with him and complained to be disturbed by Dudukudo, who demands the same thing. In order to emphasize his threat to Dudukudo, Kimgidu sends a brandishing message promising to kill him.

The next day my wife meets Dudukudo in a room of a hotel in town; it is a hotel with a private washroom. They hold casual conversation and take drinks bought by Dudukudo from the counter of the hotel. During their conversation, my wife flatters him and pretends to have great dislike on me. She promises to give him the love, but only when she is facilitated to kill me. They agree about killing me, and my wife accepts to execute the task.

In pleasure of the flattery and sweet promises from Stella, Dudukudo finds himself reckless and give a substantial amount of money to her. He vows, when I am dead, to make Stella his wife. Stella counts the money and keeps it into his pouch.

Dudukudo buys a poison and gives it to my wife, to use it in killing me. He instructs her on how to use it. "You don't have to be expert to get the poison into his blood; it only needs to take place out of your home so that you are not suspected." Dudukudo tells my wife when he gives the poison.

An intuition comes into Stella's mind that she wishes Kimgidu was around. She enters a washroom and calls him via a cell phone and asks if he can come here. When Kimgidu receives this call, he takes it as the God's blessing. He postpones all his today's schedules and promises to be around within an hour.

At one time, Dudukudo enters into a washroom and leaves a glass of drinks with Stella alone. It comes unplanned into Stella's mind when she remembers nobody has seen them when they got inside, after all she is unknown in this place. She thinks she can use this loop hole, and here is where the plot backfires to the mastermind. She approximates the time Dudukudo will spend inside the washroom and satisfied it is enough to do something.

She takes a portion of the poison and pours it into a glass of liquor left on the table by Dudukudo. When satisfied it is well mixed she picks Dudukudo's cell phone and send a message to Kimgidu: "You said you are coming, I am waiting for you here." A moment later Dudukudo returns to his place and Stella watches him, calm and relaxed.

Dudukudo takes few sips of alcohol from the glass, and it does not take long for Dudukudo to slide from his chair to the floor, he whimpers as he lies helplessly on the floor like a child denied of an access to watch cartoon. Stella drags Dudukudo with covered hands into the washroom. Then she uses Dudukudo's phone to send another message to Kimgidu, she instructs him in the same hotel and same room she is with Dudukudo. When she has done all these, she gets out and closes the door, lurks somewhere waiting for Kimgidu to arrive.

About an hour later, Kimgidu arrives at the hotel excitedly, he prowls his eyes around to search for the room he has been directed. When Stella sees Kimgidu heading to the door of the room, she moves to the hotel guard and informs him about the fight she has heard in the room entered by Kimgidu. The guard runs hurriedly into the room.

When Kimgidu opens the door of the room he finds nobody but two bottles of liquor and two glasses on a table. He presumes his host may have entered the washroom. He tries to call Stella by her name several times. The silence of the room urges him to check into the washroom. Suddenly he turns back frenziedly in response to what he sees in the washroom; here is when he finds himself face to face with the hotel guard.

In the evening, news spread all over neighboring area that the prominent businessman has been arrested for murdering his business rival in a hotel room. When we hear this, Stella and me smile and hug each other.

My Girl Called Me a Thief When I Caught Her with a Boy in Her Room.

I can hardly forget that day I almost died in the fierce hands of my fellow human beings just because of love. I don't ever want to remember that terrible evening.

Is it true that a person can learn to love somebody even if they initially didn't have feelings of love for them? On my side, although I had volunteered to fight in every way for my girl, and did every good to her as part of my efforts to try making myself the very best fit for her, in the hope that she would learn to love me, but still things ended terribly.

I am a gentleman aged 36, employed in a private company. I can say my employment enables me to provide myself with all the necessary needs. There was a girl to whom I had fallen in love, I wished she was my lover and if possible, my future wife. I made an acquaintance with the girl on one weekend when I went into a restaurant near to their college; she was with another girl who was her friend. On that day I only managed to get her phone number.

Following my subsequent conversations with her, I discovered she was still a college student. When I approached her at first she was reluctant. I visited her in their college with my car and brought her gifts and envelopes containing money. I even used her friend to help me persuade her so that she accepted my request of being my lover.

Slowly, I noticed she began to be friendly and warm to me that she accepted my invitation to go out with her. I can't precisely explain the feeling of happiness I experienced on that day I went out with her, only the two of us. I put a record in my dairy about that occasion, for the way I felt it was special and memorable to me.

I was about ten years older than her, but to me that didn't seem to be an obstacle to make our relationship flourish. I can say I had put all my hope in the girl; that she would be my wife and the mother of my children. I spent a lot of my salaries to pay for part of her college expenses and other needs. She was raised by her uncle and I made sure the uncle and her other relatives recognize me.

When she was in college, I used to ask her that we have sex considering that I had no other partner except only her. I am not sure if this sounds like I was preoccupied with the desire for sex or not, but I am just trying to be frank. The girl denied my request and showed signs of resentment to my request claiming that engaging in sex before marriage was against her religious beliefs. Although her stance somehow caused distress on my side, I had to be patient because I loved her, plus it gave me confidence concerning her behavior.

In the college, she stayed in a hostel room with another girl who was also her friend. We had a tendency to visit each other; she regularly came to my home and I went to their hostel. Sometimes I took her out with her friend. At first she welcomed me warmly even when I visited her in the hostel without prior information. But after certain interval of time, I noticed things beginning to change; the warmth she showed me when I visited her began to fade. I no longer saw the smile she showed me when I handed her a gift.

At first, I ignored the change and saw it as a normal thing, but when she reached the extent of restricting me on the time of visiting her, is when I began to be suspicious. Although she gave me the reason that her uncle had heard that I used to take her out and he was not pleased with that, but I didn't believe her and started to make a covert investigation.

Another great change I saw in her is the frequent demand for money from me. I was amazed by the fact that she claimed for too much money beyond her budget, and when I questioned her about it she only blamed me for being parsimonious and uncaring for her. Sometimes she even threatened to end our relationship if I didn't conform to her wishes. Because I loved her and felt I would be in great woe if she went away, I was willing to do anything to satisfy her.

I also got rumors from some people who knew my relationship with the girl that she used to go to clubs and engaging in casual liaison with boys in her college. I guess it was the money she demanded from me, and spent it in activities which to me she would claim sinful but to other guys it was okay. I tried to discuss with her several times and warn her about the rumors, but she declined and attributed the rumors as hearsays caused by jealousy.

There is a Saturday I prepared a rendezvous with her in a cafe; I intended to make a serious talk with her about the destiny of our relationship. There is when I openly witnessed her aversion to spend time with me. On that meeting, I tried as hard as I could to be charming to her, but whenever I talked to her she responded curtly. Even when I gave her a kiss she recoiled back resentfully, claiming she was not used to those things.

Despite her lack of enthusiasm when she was with me, I was delighted in having her near me and seeing she comes when I called her somewhere and have conversations with her. I only swallowed all her downsides I heard from other people for the sake of my satisfaction.

One evening I made a surprise visit in her hostel and found two male visitors in their room. Although she managed to welcome me inside the room, but I could easily see the sudden tension that overwhelmed them. Although my girl introduced the boys to me as her college mates, but the way in which I found them was not that of just friends; it suggested they were lovers. I got it absolutely clear that each of the girls had brought her partner into their hostel room.

You know how the hostel room looked like? It contained only two beds, a wardrobe, a table and two chairs. Here is where I found the girls and two boys locked in.

The girl I loved and fancied so very much was now in front of my eyes half naked with other boys in the room. I couldn't tolerate this; therefore I was uncontrollably filled with anger and started a fight. My girl opted to stand with the boys and turned against me. She thought she better identify herself with the boys than with me, therefore she wanted to defend them. They all shouted loud and branded me a thief as they beat me. Soon other students ran into the room and took me to the security office.

Fortunately, I possessed several identity cards, and the way I had dressed didn't resemble that of a thief. Therefore, when I was interrogated by the college guards, there was an uncertainty over the truth of the matter I was accused. I also presented to them evidences showing I was a long friend of one of the girls who lived in the hostel; this helped to justify my presence into the hostel.

The guards then turned to my girl and asked her to provide proof of their accusations. It looks like she had not prepared for the question as she and her friends couldn't mention the property I had stolen. My girl neither provided evidence that I had stolen something in their room, nor denied the fact that I and her were in a relationship, in that way I was able to avoid further beating and being sent to police station.

From that day I realized there was nothing I could do to continue my relationship with the girl, I had to carry out a tough task of learning how to live without her. The theory which is told regularly by the relationship experts that somebody can learn to love a person even if they initially didn't love them proved long to me.

I Have a Loving Heart.

At Khangaroo beach, girls swim and dance vivaciously in water, they are dressed in their skimpy beach costumes. I sit in a pub located in the beach compound and prowl to the water in the ocean. I get obsessed at the sight of roundish hips, sticky on wet skimpy pieces of cloths worn by the girls as they ostentatiously show off themselves and rock the beach atmosphere with their glamorous cheers. Ardently, I leave my drinks on a table and walk to the seashore to enjoy further view of this lively scenario.

I join a crowd of people standing along the seashore, delighting in the swimming and dancing event exhibited by the girls in the water. I move my eyes to one girl after another and thrilled with the way they are dressed and dancing, their bare bosoms covered only in flimsy brassieres.

I feel overwhelmed with excitement when my eyes land on one of the girls aged between eighteen and twenty. I fancy her desperately, with my eyes riveted to her glamorous face and her shaking wet hips. Her hips are hidden in a drenched skimpy piece of white cloth hung loosely around the hips in such a way that it reveals the strip of her lingerie. I am paralyzed as I am filled with jealousy when I see the girl embraced between arms of a boy she smooches with.

Then I see the girl with the boy come out of water holding their hands; I look at the girl saunter on the beach sand as if she doesn't want her feet touch the sand. I see her roundish hips shake in sync with the steps she makes. They pause at a man selling ice cream; they buy the ice cream and the boy walks away, leaving the girl alone. My heart beats fast as I argue with myself on whether I should approach her or not. Let me try my luck, I mutter as I move to the ice cream man and push adolescents huddled around the girl to delight with her extreme cheerfulness.

"How much?" I ask the man when I have reached him. Before he hasn't answered me, I turn to the girl standing next to the man with the ice cream she licks. "Hello girl?"

"Hi!" She replies charmingly.

The way she looks at me when she answers my greeting encourages me to talk to her, "Would you like to add more ice creams?" I ask the girl, drawing a ten thousands shillings note from my wallet. I see her sneaks a stealthy eye into my wallet which is packed with a bunch of brand-new notes.

"You can just give me the money; I will buy it on my own later." She says as she flaunts her erect breasts under a wet brassiere.

I hand the note over to the girl; she receives it with a chuckle and a flirty glance. I feel exhilarated seeing this reaction from her, I only grin with all my teeth clearly visible. "Is that your brother?" I ask, pointing to the boy she was with.

"No. He is just a boy I have met here. He asked for my company to swim together."

"Are you alone here?"" I ask again.

"I am with my friends, they are there." She answers, pointing to two girls in the water.

"Ok, me I am there in the pub. Come and let us be together if you don't mind." I invite her. Enthusiastically, she replies, "Okay, we can go.""

"I thought you should talk to your friends that you are with me." I suggest.

"Don't worry, I will inform them." She replies when she grabs my hand and leads me to the pub. "I feel elated at discovering that the girl is free and obliging."

We sit in the pub where we introduce to one another. From her introduction, I realize she is called Bituro. We drink and hold conversations in which I invite her to visit me in my hotel later, and what do you expect? My invitation is accepted with both hands. In the whole time of our conversations I see Bituro busy dialing on the buttons of her cellular phone.

"I am sending a message home that I will pass to my friend's home, therefore I will be late." She tells me.

"That's nice; we will be free to enjoy our moment." I sigh frenziedly when I fantasize the adventure of having this girl on bed.

*****

At 18 hrs, I and Bituro sojourn in a hotel room. Now everybody is accustomed to each other, I feel free to lie over her on bed. "Wait. Let us take a shower first." She tells me as she looks straight into my eyes amorously. She pulls herself away from me and springs off the bed. She strips off the beach costumes she is wearing so that she remains naked.

I drool at the sight of the naked girl; my lips palpitate as if I mumble a fudge in my mouth. As I look at her, she moves closer to me and slowly, she takes clothes off my body and she leaves me naked. I am tremendously aroused seeing that I am with this girl alone in a room, both naked.

I see Bituro jerks backward at the sight of my erection, she covers her mouth with her both palms when she sees me in this way. I stretch my arms to embrace her, but she escapes me and runs into the bathroom and locks the door.

I follow the girl at the door and knock, begging her to open.

"No please, that's too big for me!" She smiles faintly as she says this. She partly opens the bathroom door and peeps out her eyes, staring at my erection. "Let me tell you something, if you want me to open bring that handbag." She says, pointing to her handbag.

I quickly take the handbag and give it to her. "I want to apply my cosmetics after shower."" She says as she takes the handbag, and then she locks the door. She takes a small bottle in which she has put a narcotic and smears it on her nipples. She throws the bottle into the sink and then comes out of the bathroom as naked as she entered.

She moves to me and slumps onto my chest, I grab and cuddle her passionately. She moans as she aims her nipples into my mouth, I engulf the nipples, lick and suck them alternately with all the skills I can display. After about five minutes, I slide from her bosom and plunge on the floor, unconscious.

*****

Dotikomu and Mwanawane mingle with other customers in a bar of Miami hotel; they casually take sips of beer and watch a football match on a wide flat screen. A beep in Dotikomu's phone diverts their eyes from the screen. They hastily look onto the screen of the phone and see there is a message. "I have done it, the man is unconscious now. Soon I will be coming out with the stuffs, clear the way"."

After receiving the message, Dotikomu dials buttons on his phone to call the hotel receptionist. The receptionist picks the phone call, "Hello, Miami hotel here. Can I help you? She speaks in her elegant voice.

"Sorry for disturbance." Doticomu speaks in a professional tone, "I am a customer in your hotel, I am in the bar side. I need your help; can you come here for a while?

"Talk to the bar attendants, I only deal with hotel rooms; please." The receptionist replies.

"But my issue is about the rooms and I can't leave here because I have delicate properties." Dotikomu insists. The receptionist is ready to favor her customer even by making minor deviation from work rules. She decides to leave her office and go to the bar to attend her customer.

While Dotikomu talks to the receptionist in the bar, Mwanawane sends a message to Bituro in the room to inform that the receptionist has vacated her place, therefore she can pass freely.

"I was asking if we can get two self contained rooms for our visitors arriving from Nairobi tonight." Dotikomu lies to the receptionist when she has come to the bar.

"Unfortunately all rooms are occupied, we are sorry." The receptionist tells him.

"Dotikomu feigns a regretful look after hearing this, "this is truly a misfortune. Our visitors liked your hotel so much; I don't know what we will do now." He speaks when him and Mwanawane stand up and go.

In the hotel room, Bituro collects anything she sees valuable to her; the wallet containing bunch of notes, a laptop, a digital camera and two smart phones. She takes all my clothes and puts them into a bag, and then she walks out.

*****

I return to my consciousness at 22 hrs at night and find myself lying alone on bed, in my hotel room. I sit upright, stretch and yawn frequently. I rub my face and remember I was with a girl in the room. With a wrinkled face, I turn around as though to search for her, "Bituro." I call.

I look at a coffee table where I had put my two smart phones and find it is empty. An alarming suspicion hits in my head when I throw my eyes to a hanger where I suspended my clothes and those of Bituro, and find they are not there. My laptop, clothes, and my wallet with 300,000 shillings in it have gone!

For a moment, I put my hand in my waist and stand stunned. With only a boxer in my body, I open the door and rush to reception office, "Hey, there is a thief in your hotel!" I shout as I run through the corridor to the reception office.

At the reception office, I grasp the receptionist firmly on her shoulders with my both hands and shake her violently, "You are thieves! Bring my properties back or I will show you who I am." I shout and lift her up so that she hangs from my hands.

"What has happened? Calm down brother?" The receptionist complains, struggling to pull herself free.

Luckily, other customers run to us and intervene. They help pull the receptionist from my fierce hands. When we have calmed, I, the receptionist, and the hotel guard go to my room to prove my accusations.

"It is not possible for a person to go out of the hotel with all those properties and you are here, you must be involved in the plot." I continue shouting throwing my arms in air furiously.

"You claim your properties have been stolen but the door is not broken. How did the thief get in?" The hotel guard asks me. I don't answer him, but only breathe rapidly with sweat drenching my clothes.

"Did you enter with somebody in the room?" The receptionist asks me another question.

"And where is my girl Bituro? You have stolen my properties, as if not enough you have stolen even my girl!" Instead of answering their questions, I still cast my accusations to the hotel workers.

"You must be drunk! We don't even know the girl you are talking about." The guard tells me, showing he is irritated by my remarks.

"No. Bituro cannot take my properties and leave me like this. May be somebody else got in when she went out and stole my properties." I look down to contemplate. "Could Bituro really steal my properties? But why she left without telling me." I ask myself these questions when all people here are silent, looking at me. "What will I do now? All my belongings have gone!" Then I ask the hotel workers, "Is there anybody who knows this girl?"

"You are asking us while it's you who came with the girl? Where did you take her?" The receptionist asks me.

I finally begin to narrate how I met the girl at Khangaroo beach and invite her to come with me in the hotel. After he has heard the details, the hotel guard says, "Now I understand; you must have succumbed into a trap of the Dudukudo gang. I see you don't know this town properly. You have to ask your hosts before you make friendship with people." The hotel guard says, he turns to the receptionist as if to clear himself from blames of irresponsibility. Then he goes on telling me, "In this town there is a gang called Dudukudo; when you mentioned Khangaroo beach there I begin to comprehend the type of girl you welcome into your hotel room. During weekends they crowd the beach to hunt for people with valuable properties to steal."

"I spend some minutes to stay quiet and calm down, I see I have to accept the situation. "Let me talk to my hosts about the incident so that we report to the police." Finally I suggest. But because it is already night, we agree to do this tomorrow morning.

*****

The next morning I and my host who is also my office mate, report to the police about the theft. My host and some of police officers here are friends so they attend us quickly and kindly.

"You say you firstly met the girl at Khangaroo beach, did you capture her name?" The police officer asks me when he takes details about the incident.

"Yes, her name is Bituro." I reply.

"You say you were with her in your hotel room, how then she managed to escape without your notice?" The officer whose name is Gillard asks again.

"For sure, that is what confuses me. But what I can remember is that she went into the bathroom to bath, after that she came to me, on bed. Thereafter I don't remember what happened until I came into my conscious when she had left with my properties.

Gillard asks again, "When you entered into the hotel room was there any of the hotel attendants around?"

"Yes, there was a hotel receptionist and the hotel guard."

"Why do you think, all these didn't see the girl when she came out of your room with a bag from their hotel?" The police officer asks.

"That is what surprises me; I can hardly believe if Bituro really stole my properties because if you saw the girl, you wouldn't believe it; she is very innocent."

Gillard spends some few minutes to ponder about something. Then he nodes his head as a sign he is satisfied with something. "I think we need to talk with the receptionist and the hotel guard." Then, Gillard and Sydney in their plain clothes and I embark in a police vehicle to Miami hotel.

*****

The police vehicle stops at the gate of Miami hotel, we drop from the vehicle and lead inside the hotel where we are received by the hotel guard. "Welcome," The guard says and leads us to the reception office.

"We are police officers from the central police station; we have come to interrogate you about theft which happened in your hotel last night." Gillard gives an introduction to the hotel workers, and shows his identity card. Then he says, "We need to talk to the hotel manager."

The hotel manager hurries into the reception office when he is informed about the coming of the police. The police conduct an interview with the hotel manager. "I think you recognize this man as your customer for some days now?" Gillard asks the hotel manager when he holds my right shoulder.

"Yes, we recognize him." The manager confirms.

"And you are aware about the theft which occurred in his hotel room last night?"

"Yes, he reported to us immediately after the incident."

"And what actions did you take when you received the report?" The police officer asks and writes the details into his dairy.

"First of all, we insist our customers to submit their valuable possessions at the reception office so that we recognize them, but this customer didn't do so. We are surprised to hear that his properties are missing while door of his room is not broken, and he has admitted that he allowed a strange girl into his room, and the girl left without his notice."

"When your customer hired a room did you notify him about those regulations?"

"Yes, he was notified by the receptionist. Also the rules are available in each hotel room for customers to be familiarized." The hotel manager says and show a paper with the rules which is stuck on the wall of the reception office.

"Where are the hotel attendant and the hotel guard who were on duty when the incident happened?" Gillard asks.

"Here they are." The manager replies, referring to the workers sitting next to him.

Gillard turns to the hotel receptionist and asks, "From the time your customer got into his hotel room until this problem was discovered is there any moment you left your work place?"

"Myself I didn't leave my place." The guard replies, while the receptionist spends some seconds rubbing her chin, she allows a moment to remind herself, and then she says, "Yes I left, about two times."

"Where did you go? And did you leave anybody at the reception?"

"There was a time I went into the toilet, and the other time I went to attend a customer in the bar. I didn't see the need to leave a substitute here because it only took short time." The receptionist explains.

Detective Sydney interrupts and asks, "Why did you go to serve a bar customer while it is not your area? And, how did you know that the customer needs a service while you were at the reception?"

"He called me through a phone and said he couldn't leave his belongings alone there, to show the customer our good service and because he was just few pace from here, I thought it would be better if I go."

The detective shakes his head when he hears this account, as if dissatisfied. He notes something in his diary, then he asks, "Then what did he tell you when you went?"

"He asked for a room for his visitors who were arriving from Nairobi, but unfortunately the rooms were all occupied, so he didn't get it."

"Can you describe a little about the person? How did he look like and if whether he was accompanied with somebody else or he was alone."

"He was accompanied with one man; he is black, aged between 25 and 30 years. He wore a black trouser, a white short-sleeved shirt and a red tie." The receptionist explains.

"The way you found him did you see he possessed any bag or did he look like he was busy that he was unable to follow you to your office? And do you think there was any chance that the girl used to escape other than that? These questions from the detective awaken the receptionist, it's like she has managed to unravel a puzzle. She only gawks, staring the police officer.

When a brief moment of silence has passed, detective Gillard instructs the receptionist to search for the phone number used by that customer in the call history of her phone.

The receptionist searches in her cellular phone the number used by the customer by comparing the time when he received his call. When she finds the number she gives it to the detective. The detective takes two other numbers in the call history, one before and one after the desired number.

After satisfied with what they wanted, the cops take the receptionist and the hotel guards to police station for further investigation. Then the police allow me to go home but they promise to call me anytime if necessary.

*****

When they finish their interview at Miami hotel, Corporal Gillard and Sydney lock the hotel guard and the receptionist up at the police station and sit in their office to review the details they collected from their interviewees. "Our task ahead is to identify the person who possesses the number which called the receptionist."

"I guess they must be the Dudukudo gang. You see their ingenuity; the person who called the receptionist must have communicated with the girl who was in the hotel room with the victim. He called the receptionist to vacate her from his place so that the girl escaped easily after stealing." Corporal Sydney tells his colleague Gillard.

"I wonder where the hotel guard was when the girl escaped." Gillard asks.

"I think even if the guard saw the girl he would not suspect anything because he knew there were other workers in charge inside who would have dealt with her." Corporal Sydney suggests.

"But do you remember according to the receptionist the person who called her dressed in good manner, do you think this kind of person would have been involved in such crime?" Corporal Gillard asks.

"You talk as if you are not a detective. Don't you know that criminals are also intelligent, and sometimes more than the police. Do you expect them to enter in that hotel with their ghetto manners?" Corporal Sydney replies with a faint giggle.

When they check the registered user of the number in the respective telephone company, they find a name and picture of a man who is in their black list of criminals; he is a suspected member of the Dudukudo gang. Later on, the police go to suspect's home without prior notice in order to conduct a search. There they find him with other three people including two girls. They also catch some properties hidden in their ghetto.

I receive a phone call from corporal Gillard to go to the police station where I am required to identify the suspects who are detained in the station after their arrest with the properties they stole. "Bituro!" I mutter and gape surprised when I see my girl in the lock up. Then I turn to the police officers, "What has this girl done, she does not deserve here." I say compassionately, pointing my finger to the girl.

"We found her with his colleagues hiding in a ghetto with stolen things, come and check if you will find yours." Detective Gillard tells me when I look at him and show my concern for the girl. Then he beckons me and walks to the store used to keep things caught with thieves as evidences.

"You have found only these? I don't see my laptop and two smart phones." I tell detective Gillard when I have verified my properties and found some missing.

"They will tell where they are." Corporal Gillard replies, and then he leads me into his office. In the office I insist Bituro be released on grounds that she is too innocent to suffer the distress of lock up. I am even ready to bribe the officers to insist my request.

"Don't you want to get back your properties? Don't you want the law be enforced?" Detective Gillard asks me, I see him smiles gently.

I scratch my fore head and grimace, "Let these wicked suffer it, but leave the girl free." I propose.

I see Gillard laughs, and then he rubs his nose and say, "The law can't be biased."

Sydney who was quiet for long time says, "May be if you tell us not to file the case, you can do that if you wish, and that will be the end of our work."

"It's okay, if that will free the girl." I say quickly, "I would rather lose all my belongings than let my heart suffer by putting this girl in jeopardy." When I say this, my face is overwhelmed with pity and feelings of guilt. The police now have no other option except that of releasing the suspects.

Sources of Violence in Romantic relationships.

Violence in romantic relationships has been defined in different ways by psychologists and sociologists; for instance one of the definitions is that: Violence in romantic relationship is a tendency of one partner to control the relationship physically, psychologically and sexually (Gökdağ, 2015).

There is a close relationship between jealousy and violence in romantic relationship. Andac Demirtas-Madran-a Profesor of social psychology from the University of Baskent-Turkey writes in his article titled Understanding Coping with Romantic Jealousy: Major Theoretical Approaches that in romantic relationship, jealousy is a concept which results from a combination of emotions manifested by an individual when they encounter a perceived threat which would end or destroy a relationship that is considered important.

Couples show jealousy because they perceive a threat of losing either the relationship or self esteem. Men show jealousy in order to protect self-esteem, while women show jealousy in order to protect the relationships. In an effort to protect their interest (relationship or self-esteem), couples use various ways such as punishing, refraining from providing needs, et cetera.

Another reason for violence in romantic relationships is the painful feelings perceived by one side when they anticipate a breakup with a loved one (Gökdağ, 2015). There are certain feelings which accompany jealousy; for example anger, fear, envy, grief, guilt, etc. In order to get rid of these feelings, a victim would opt to eliminate/escape the source those feelings by either harming it.

In 2017, researchers Nancy Consuelo *et al*, from the department of psychology, University of El Bosque, Bogota-Colombia wrote an article titled *A systematic review of romantic jealousy in relationships* in which they mention sources of jealousy in romantic relationships. One of the sources which were mentioned was lack of self-esteem among couples.

Review of publications from various researchers mentions other sources of romantic jealousy like overdependence of one side of couples to another, lack of self-confidence, too much loving, failure to study partner's feelings, as contributing factors in romantic jealousy and hence violence in relationships.

People can rely on different ways to deal with romantic jealousy as proposed by researchers. For instance, according to Professor Andac Demirtas-Madran, one way of dealing with jealousy is that which can make the relationship even stronger; this include open conversation between couples (they should be open about their feelings to their partners).

The Confused Seducer.

I wonder if there is any male reading this article has ever seduced a woman, longing to know what did they reply, did they reject or accept? What other observations you noticed from their face?

Here is a discourse about what happens in the surroundings of couples' romantic conversations. This is based on mostly, people's testimony plus the writer's personal view on the realm of seduction.

Most female humans get excited when they are seduced; the excitement is proved from the gestures and other forms of responses shown by females when seduced. Unfortunately, this excitement has sometimes been misinterpreted by male seducers who tend to confuse it with acceptance.

For females, being seduced is something like of good news to them; they get assured of the status of their beauty, that they are beautiful and valuable women. This in turn generates hope in them of getting prospective valuable male partners, or hope of acquiring prestige from other people regarding their beauty. This good hope manifests as smile, laughter or any other related gesture.

One evening when I was seated on the shore of a beach with my friends, a very pleasing lady passed in front of us. She was dressed in a transparent miniskirt which revealed pink lingerie and she only covered her breasts in her remaining body.

All of us were overwhelmed by the girl and we couldn't resist ourselves from talking about her. As our discussion became wider, one of our friends began to tell his story about a certain girl to whom he had fallen in love. He explained how he tried to seduce the girl and that the girl also showed signs of love for him but still she was reluctant to get into sexual affair with him.

"How do you know that you are also loved by the girl?" We asked him.

"I just know it because whenever I approach her she becomes joyous and smiles at me, if she didn't love me she wouldn't show all these". Our friend replied confidently.

"Why then do you think she doesn't accept your request for making love with her if you think she loves you? We further asked him.

He replied "That's what confuses me; sometimes I become angry thinking that she is trying to play with my nerves".

"Oh, maybe you are confusing yourself for your tendency to attribute the girl's smile and positive reactions to her willingness for love, why are you preoccupied with the desire of making love with her? Probably she truly loves you except that she is not ready to engage in sex with you."

"This hurts me so much; I even have lost the appetite to the extent of developing ulcers. I am afraid this is going to be worse" he lamented.

"This guy must be really confused" I whispered to a man who seated close to me.

Everybody can be Loved.

I will use the term 'Love seeker' to refer to a person who looks for love, or wants to be loved. Also, I will use the term 'Donor of love' to refer to a person from whom love is desired, or a person who should give out love to the love seeker.

Just like a candle, burning slowly in the dark, love cheers the hopeless, and consoles the sad. As it has been written by Pennington et al., (1999, page 234-236), animals put a great deal of their attention in love; whether it is a normal love, like that of mother to her child *philia* or romantic love *'eros'*. Furthermore, Gross (2009), argues that, people show love to others when they receive attraction first, (See the Social Exchange theory, on page 484).

Different people have different ways by which they are attracted, thus everybody has a way(s) by which can attract someone, and be loved by them. If a love seeker wants to be loved, they need to struggle to attract their donor of love.

According to the Greek Philosopher, Plato, love is the desire to possess goodness perpetually/permanently. Goodness is always loved; therefore, if a love seeker wants to be loved, they first need to struggle to acquire goodness. When a love seeker succeeds to acquire goodness, it will persuade donor of love desire to posses and/or utilize that goodness, and therefore love them.

When goodness from love seeker pleases the donor of love, they will feel this pleasure, and associate it with its source (i.e. the love seeker). This will leave the donor of love longing to enjoy further and other pleasure hidden in the love seeker.

However, it is difficult to rely on goodness in order to win love. This is due to several reasons; first, sometimes it is difficult for the love seeker to know what exactly would please the donor of love in order that they donate love. This is one of problematic areas when it comes to building relationships.

Secondly, there are several goodness that is desired in a relationship; for example on bed, caring, security, physical attraction etc; it is not easy for a love seeker to struggle and have all kinds of goodness which are needed to attract, satisfy, and keep the donor of love.

Third, people's perceptions about goodness change (Pennington *et al.*, 1999, page 234.), today they may perceive something as good and be attracted by it, but in the future that thing may lose its taste as perceived before.

If all the 'struggle for love' strategies fail, the love seeker will have to choose one option, either quit that slavery, or surrender as a slave under the captivity of the donor of love, provided that they enjoy that slavery.

When the love seeker strives for love from their donor of love, at the same time they aim for their own happiness/joy; they feel joy when they realize that their donor of love also loves them back. Love seeker can sacrifice to surrender as slaves of their donor of love when they feel joy to love regardless they are loved back or not.

Females Carry Beauty but Do not Own It.

I presume you might be wondering how this sounds, to put it clear, this title does not imply that females should be misused for sexual indulgence. I just want to show how attractive instincts of females serve as an honorable privilege of the almighty creation to societies. Also, remind readers who are in romantic relationship on how they should mutually treat each other, for the sake of the relationship.

An attractive partner is an important prerequisite to provoke love. Remember that the way people are attracted by others varies, so everybody can attract someone in their own way(s). It is males who initiate sex process, thus they should be attracted first so that they set a way for its occurrence (Buss and Larsen, 2005, page 515 & 517). This implies that attractive qualities are more confined to females than males.

Females were created with external attractive appearances for both biological and social reasons. Philosophically, the beauty possessed in females is not their personal belonging; they do not own the beauty even though they carry it. Females are used just as a medium to carry it.

The responsibility of females is to relish and share the beauty they possess to societies, by showing love and care to other people, especially the hopeless and inferiors. By doing this, females will be playing their paramount position as mother of societies.

Apart from being a prerequisite toward successful romantic relationship, this beauty and/or aesthetic of females is important to other members of the society (e.g. their male partners) as a relief against social stresses and aggressions.

If this beauty was absent, or if it was not shared in societies, it would be difficult for people to get relief from various constraints they face in their day to day life. This would lead to an overstressed, aggressive society even worse than it looks today.

However, it is unpleasant and inhuman for females to use their beauty and aesthetics privileges as a tool to mistreat the community in which they belong. In some occasions, females have been forced to use their femininity as a tool of defense or economic benefit. They use it to overcome difficult situations they face, and gain prestige, security or economic triumphs.

Love and Social Disorders.

Animals are created with inborn energy to procreate or produce young individuals, and they utilize or exude this energy by practicing sexual intercourse. If this energy is not fully utilized or exuded, it will be lost in other biological or psychological forms, some of which are violent against animal itself.

According to Rosenhan & Seligman, (1995, page 472), when animals are sexually dissatisfied, they develop symptoms which may manifest in other forms, which are quite non sexual; for example morbidity, perversion et cetera. Personally, I presume that, the desire for sex was built in as one of life instincts in animals due to the role of procreation that was entitled to them by the God.

Let me ask you this question; how does human mind deal with the desire for sex? Or I can put it in this way, what is the relationship between animal's sexual desire and his intelligence? To be understood easily, let me use an example of hunger; how does animal operates to eliminate the need for food? How does the animal deals with hunger?

If you have asked yourself these questions, you might have realized that, hunger can only be dealt with by satisfying it; otherwise you will be buried within a very short life span. That is how life instincts are; they cannot be eliminated or resisted by intelligence.

As it is for hunger, the same applies for sexual desire. The sexual desire of potent animals cannot be resisted by intelligence, it can only be dealt with by its satisfaction with an instant, or at least delayed sexual prospect. When sexual desire gets into our bodies, it suppresses our mental strength so that we become reckless disciples of sex (Soble, A. et al. 2002). In my view, probably, what can intelligence do in sex, is moderate it so that it is practiced in humanly and determined way.

Life is composed of various conditions and matters, these occur as multitude of units in the whole of the life system. These units are intra-and-interconnected by bonds. The bonds which connect the units of life themselves are many, and spread throughout the whole sphere of life. Therefore, there is a system of units of life, and a system of bonds which connect those units. This shows how life is a complex system.

Human being lives as a victim subjected to a disorder in systems of life surrounding him. This disorder is brought by the fact that life is complex, and hence its control is complicated as well. Although man tries to formulate orders so that to mitigate the effects of this disorder, still the orders seem to be overwhelmed, leaving life contaminated with chaos.

Love, as one of units which form the system of life, seems to be affected by this disorder. The disorder in the system of life has brought frustrated and aggressive animals that progressively lose the instinct to love and become substituted with instinct of hate, killing and suicide. An animal with aggression has no interest to contemplate about love; this affects the manner in which romantic relationship is treated.

Sexual-social Crises in Romantic Relationships.

There is a rumor, or I should say myth, among girls that, if a man sleeps with a girl before marriage, there is a possibility for the man to lose interest to marry her, because he will have tasted and experienced the feel of the girl, and thus lose appetite for her. This could be a challenge which contributes to jeopardize strong relationship between couples.

This myth of most girls is not a mere hearsay; it has logic which is based on reality. These girls know well their male counterparts since they live with them; they know that there are some of men who are preoccupied with tendency to go into casual relationship with many girls.

The bodies of ladies are built in such a way that they can attract others just by looking at them; they have tempting appearances on both their faces and shapes. Some of men fail to resist or cope with temptations brought by external attraction of the ladies; they may be easily influenced by the wish to engage in casual sexual relationship with the ladies who attract them.

When these men become infatuated with outward attractions of women, they need them only for immediate use. As a result, their female mates see men as playboys; they become frustrated as their expectations in the sexual relationship are not met. In the long run, this may jeopardize courtship and subsequent marriages.

Men and women have dissimilar interest regarding the purpose of getting into a sexual relationship, when women expose themselves at the eyes of men for the purpose of creating a long lasting relationship; men abuse this opportunity by using the women contrary to what the women wished.

The disparity in motive for getting into a sexual relationship between men and women creates what I can call a sexual-social crisis between the two sexes. Women become plagued with indignation due to what they perceive as unfair treatment from their male counterparts. Even if the relationships reach to marriage stage, they are still haunted by the sexual-social crises; you will hear men and women accuse each other for being the source of infidelity in marriages.

Research is required to find out the primary perpetrator of the infidelity in marriages, whether it's the men or women. It should also help to discover if whether sex of an individual or other biological or genetic attributes have effects to determine whether the individual will be a betrayer or not.

Because women are a huge and important group in communities, there is no way societies can avoid consequences which result from bad attitudes of women about men, and hence bad sexual social relationship between them. It is a challenge which faces the women, but its effects return to the whole community, including men themselves.

Strength and Confidence as Important Qualities in Romantic Relationships.

In their research about physical attractiveness, Frederick and Haselton (2007), report that women rate muscular men as sexier, more physically dominant and volatile; women rate muscular men as more sexually desirable than both non-muscular men and very muscular men.

Furthermore, women like the physical strength of males just because it pleases to their senses (Rosenhan& Seligman, 1995). In my view, I can say that, just like the way males admire breasts, hips and other features of women, the same reason makes females admire the muscular bodies of males.

For those who believe in Bible, in Genesis 3:16, the God put a woman under her man, (I know there are scriptures similar to this in books of other religions). But what qualities does a man need in order to maintain this status entitled to him by the God? How can a man undertake this privilege and manage the relationship with his woman if he is not strong?

Men would be more successful in attracting women if their strength is combined with confidence, they should have strength and confidence in a cause -and -effect relationship. This means that, they need to be men who are strong, and this strength is a cause of their confidence. When they have males who are strong and confident, females feel secured.

While the relationship between physical strength of a man and his sexual efficiency can be justified by logics of biology, the relationship between confidence of a man and preference in sexual relationship seems to be merely social; this means that some women would want to flaunt to others that, they can conquer the hearts of confident men, just with their beauty.

In my view, the strength needed by men as a prerequisite for being preferred by females can be categorized into two types; physical strength and social strength.

The physical strength is the muscular bodies of men. Males with muscular bodies are viewed and believed to have high capacity to withstand the sexual intercourse for long time without being fatigued. However, this does not necessarily mean that they are good in sexual structures.

In addition, there are some females who feel pleasure being cuddled between muscular bodies of males, it facilitates their sexual arousal as the touch of the arms and chest of muscular bodies is more catchy and sensible.

The social strengths of males, which can be used as an advantage for winning the hearts of some females, is the statuses that males hold relative to others in the society. It can be economic, social or any other superiority (Larsen &Buss, 2005). These females would prefer to benefit, associate and identify themselves with the superiority of males; they would do this by offering 'anything' they have to the superior males.

The Use of Science and Art to Improve Romantic Relationship.

What does it need to be a competent person in romantic relationship, is it the skills in science, or art? There are certain prior stages which should be achieved before arriving at the last stage which is intended by partners when they embark into a relationship.

Examples of these stages are attraction, seduction, and others. And these constitute art. There is a close relationship between the act of intercourse between lovers, and those stages which precede it. The sexual attraction which occurs between two partners, all the troubles of seducing a partner are brought about by art; science joins in the subsequent stages, although it may still be complemented by art.

Art is an important companion in order for the love between two partners to exist longer. The efforts and behaviors partners will exhibit towards each other, and for their sexual relationship, is art. These behaviors play a great role in creating aesthetics necessary to infatuate science, and hence trigger it to take place.

An animal with exposure in various aspects of science related to romance, which in this article I will call it romantic science, has an added advantage to benefit from sexual relationship. Knowledge of issues like mechanism of sexual arousal, sensitive parts of a partner, housekeeping procedures of the sexual structures, and others, are romantic science, which work best if they complement the art.

In addition, all the events which take place in the body, and which lead to ovulation, arousal, erection, and consequent ejaculation, constitute romantic science. But, in order that they bring desirable effects as intended by partners, they should work concurrently with some sort of art.

By reading this article, I hope my readers will have realized that, art and science need to operate in cooperation in a romantic relationship.

Therefore, I expect that lovers will take efforts to improve their knowledge and skills in both.

Why Betrayals in Romantic Relationships is a Common Practice?

When the word sex is mentioned, it tends to send rude impression in the ears of listeners. But we forget that it has very important role, biologically, psychologically and physiologically. Due to its importance, if partners do not satisfy both their physiological and psychological needs of sex, there is a high likelihood that one partner or both will betray or contemplate for betrayal.

The psychological needs of sex require a partner who attracts/pleases their mate while such thing is not necessary in the physiological needs of sex. According to Buss & Larsen (2005), personality plays a key role in what people want in a marriage partner.

Furthermore, a male and a female may engage in sex while there is no feeling of mutual attraction between them, especially when they need to carter for their physiological needs of sex, for example, when partners engage in sex in order to have a child.

Both males and females have problems in satisfying their psychological needs of sex, one of reasons for this is that psychology itself is wide as far as interaction with different people is concerned. When males and females interact in various occasions, sometimes there may happen unexpected events of mutual attraction between new males and new females (Gross, 2009).

In addition, as it has been argued above, people need to be attracted before they embark into a sexual relationship with a partner, and be able to keep it. And, it is difficult for an individual to be precise in every way as desired by their partners. For instance, they cannot satisfy in all aspects like caring, security, physical attraction, on bed, etc.

Furthermore, people's perceptions about goodness change (Pennington et al., 1999, page 234.), today they may perceive something as good and be attracted by it, but in the future that thing may lose its taste as perceived before.

Think of how situation will be for partners who have a long distance relationship, considering that there are natural processes related to procreation operating in their bodies. The physiological need of procreation is accomplished with the aid of certain natural biological mechanisms which take place within the bodies of animals.

Examples of these mechanisms are *Oogenesis, spermatogenesis, ovulation* etc, which lead to accumulation of semen or ova in the genitalia of the partners. The accumulated semen and ova switches on another physiological stage which manifests as an irresistible urge to purge the accumulated materials, in psychology, this is what is known as libido.

If partners are not well trained on how to cope with situations of separation between them what should we expect? All these behaviors have huge contribution in determining how people would behave in romantic relationship.

There is Beauty in Everybody.

Author Helena Motoh, a Professor at the Science and Research Centre in Slovenia, writes in her article, quoting a Chinese philosopher known as Confucius that, everybody is beautiful in their own way, but not everybody can find it. Furthermore, beauty is no quality in things themselves; it exists merely in the mind which contemplates them; it is a property that lies in the beholder (Cascales, 2017; *Stanford Encyclopedia of Philosophy*).

These philosophical quotations tend to imply that there should be someone who can make a perfect couple with another; now, where is the problem? Why do we hear incidence of betrayals and violence in romantic relationships?

Probably, the problem is the difficulty for a person to recognize the moment and location where they can find someone who matches them, so that they meet and initiate a desirable and true relationship.

Also, these quotations imply that the beauty possessed by people differs from person to person; and it is this beauty which creates love between a person and their fellows. This love brings people closer in order to build relationship between them.

Buss & Larsen (2005, page 515 & 517), argue that it is males who normally initiate sexual relationship by approaching ladies, this statement implies that males needs to be attracted first so that they can initiate that relationship.

External or internal attraction is important for people to embark into a relationship, therefore, it is important for lovers to keep themselves attractive in order to provoke and sustain positive feelings among themselves.

Why True Love is Hard to Find?

Psychologists and philosophers have given different meanings of the word love or Eros or Romantic love, as it has been used in the realm of romantic relationship. In order to explain this topic, I will use an online article which deals with Plato's theory about love. This article was published by Lydia Amir, a professor of philosophy from Israel.

In her article titled *'Plato's theory of Love: Rationality as Passion'*, published in 2001, professor Lydia Amir explains the meaning of love, quoting a prominent Greek philosopher known as Plato that, love is the desire for the perpetual possession of the good.

'The good' referred to by Plato in this theory, is not external appearance; rather, it is human's highest capacity of thinking. When a person has attained this capacity of thinking, he possesses the ability to love things by looking them internally, and not their external appearance.

According to Plato, in order for a person to possess goodness they first need to be a philosopher (i.e. to have the highest capacity of thinking). Plato continues arguing that, the love perceived by being attracted by external appearance is not real/true; it is just a stage towards fulfillment of a desire to possess goodness. That is why a person loves the one person, after a certain time they leave them and love another; this is because they are still in search (has not yet attained) the goodness they desire to possess.

When a person attains the highest level of thinking, they acquire ability to recognize the secret of beauty hidden in everything. And this is the highest level in loving; but it is rare for people to reach this level of thinking, and be able to acquire/possess beauty.

Professor Lydia Amir (2001), writes further that human being perform their activities by being motivated by desire to acquire beauty/goodness. In addition, human beings know that they have a desire, but they do not know who will fulfill their desire.

Because they do not know that all their activities are motivated to the possession of beauty, when a human being loves somebody, does not know for sure that there is where they will find beauty; as a result they love different people, or they love improperly.

On the other hand, another ancient Greek philosopher known as Aristotle believed that true love is a new soul dwelling between two lovers. True love needs two lovers who conjoin their souls so that they bear new soul which live forever between them.

Now, let us turn to the real life we live today; how many of us can reach the highest level of thinking proposed by philosopher Plato so that we love things internally and find love in everything? As human beings, we differ in the way we think, we feel, in our needs et cetera, how can we have a single soul which live between two lovers as proposed by philosopher Aristotle? These are some of questions which were not answered by these philosophers in their theories.

How to Deal with Infidelity or Betrayals in Romantic Relationships.

Researchers Stephen M. Drigotas et al from Southern Methodist University, Texas-USA, conducted a research in the year 1999 about factors which contribute to dating infidelity, I find several arguments in their research work which are relevant to matters of betrayals which I want to show here, and which occur in romantic relationships.

In short, among other factors, their research work mentions lack of commitment among partners/couples as one of reasons which can contribute to acts of infidelity in romantic relationships. In my view, commitment in a romantic relationship involves couples being ready, and willing to sacrifice all that could jeopardize the relationship, and embark into the relationship for themselves, their partner, and the relationship itself.

I can further paraphrase what Drigotas and his fellows write in their work that when contemplating to practice infidelity, committed couples consider long term effects of their practices; for instance breakup, hurting their partners etc. Also, committed couples tend to invest their time and material things in their relationships; and would not want to lose these investments if the relationship breaks up as a result of infidelity (betrayal). Thus, they would try to be faithful in order to protect their investment.

Satisfaction in romantic relationship is one of the requirements in order to develop good level of commitment in the relationships. Satisfaction heavily depends on whether a partner receives from the relationship what they expected from it when they embarked into it at the start. In other words I can say that dissatisfaction in a relationship can be one of criteria for lowering the level of commitment of a partner, and thus bring them into infidelity/betrayal.

Other researchers, Cindy M. Meston and David M. Buss from the department of psychology, University of Texas-USA, in their online article titled '*Why Humans Have Sex?*" published in the year 2007, provide an account on both physiological and psychological reasons on why humans need romantic relationship.

One of the physiological reasons mentioned is in order to have a child. Therefore, if couples who are in a relationship cannot fulfill either of the two reasons (for example to bear a child), then there is a high possibility for betrayal to occur.

Physiology is a mechanism of body functions (Luciano, Sherman and Vander, 1985, pg 1). For instance, when the body functions to produce sperms or *ova*, that is body physiology; this mechanism involves stages like *Oogenesis, Spermatogenesis, Ovulation* etc (Luciano, Sherman and Vander, 1985, pg 553 & 568). These stages lead to production of sperms or ova depending on sex of a person.

After production of sperms or ova (eggs), the body will want to utilize them for the intended purpose of producing another creature, here is where an individual feels sexual desire; in psychology this sensation is called *Libido*.

Another reason for betrayal in romantic relationship is explained by author Pennington in his book called *Social Psychology*, published in the year 1999, page 234, that people's feelings about beauty change. Today they may perceive something to be beautiful, and be attracted by it, but in future that thing may lose the previously perceived beauty.

As I have mentioned in other pages of this book, Professor Lydia Amir (2001), writes by quoting philosopher Plato that a human being performs their activities by being motivated by desire to possess beauty. Human beings know that they have desires, but they do not know who will fulfill their desires.

Even in relationships, a human may love somebody; but because they do not know that all their activities are motivated to possess beauty/ goodness, they do not know exactly that there is where they will find the beauty they are looking for; as a result they may find that they fall in love to different people, and thus fall into betrayal.

Think about how the situation may be for couples who are in a long distance relationship; if these people do not have adequate knowledge on how to live in such a relationship, what should we expect? All cases shown above can have great contribution on either faithfulness or betrayals in relationships.

How can couples in relationships deal with betrayals? To know the level of commitment of a partner at the beginning of the relationship, the way a partner invests for the relationship, can be used to predict how they value it, thus they will protect it by avoiding betrayals (Drigotas et al, 1999).

Couples should struggle to maintain aspects which created commitment in partners when the relationship began; this will also help to sustain the commitment. These aspects can either be material resources, emotional, social attributes or otherwise. Sometimes a partner may practice infidelity (betrayal) just because they want to retaliate a real or perceived infidelity (Drigotas et al, 1999). Therefore, it is important for couples to avoid/clear practices/situations which create wrong impression that there is betrayal (while in reality there is no such intention).

According to professor Demirtas-Madran H. A., in her online article titled *Understanding Coping with Romantic Jealousy: Major Theoretical Approaches*, people evaluate their relationships as more satisfying and durable when their outcomes (rewards, punishments, and costs) are more or less equal. The more dependent an individual is on the relationship, the more likely they will be jealous, since they have more to lose.

Let me use this example; if one partner prefers to go to nightclub to dance, if they prohibit the other to do the same, jealousy is likely to rise. The prohibited may feel that they are betrayed, and may want to revenge.

The Root cause of Crises in Romantic Relationships.

Two ancient Greek philosophers Socrates and Plato had similar views about evils; both of them believed that ignorance is the root of all evils (Pecorino, 2001; Pigliucci, 2011). This belief is still relevant even in crises which occur in modern romantic relationships. Nowadays, most of crises which occur in romantic relationships are initiated or intensified by failure of couples to understand why one partner acts or speaks something.

Sometimes it happens in romantic relationships that one partner acts or speaks something for good reason; but it is wrongly interpreted by their lover; if the lover (the wrong interpreter) is not ready to ignore or accede humbly to the acts or remarks, they may want to revenge; but actually the revenge is only due to wrong interpretation.

For a partner who lacks knowledge on how to deal with acts, behaviors or remarks from their spouse might rely on taking harmful revenge, or only appease and stay lenient to the offensive spouse.

Also, inability to understand human nature contributes greatly to initiate or intensify crises in relationships. People who are in relationships need to acquire knowledge on how humans react to different situations or circumstances. By knowing this it will be easy for lovers to know/find the right decision to take when facing a crisis in their relationships.

Sometimes couples who are in relationships may be unhappy with their lover, but reluctant or not knowing how to speak it openly; may be because the matter is too disgusting or shameful to speak. Instead, the unhappy gives remarks of condemnation while they hide their grievances, which affect the relationship subtly.

In order to avoid crises which arise from casual arguments, it is important for lovers to refrain from showing quick responses or actions;

they need to take time to understand the basis for remarks or actions, behaviors shown by their lovers. They should be ready to ask twice from people who speak or give the remark in question. Staying quiet enables the mind to have time to study and analyze situations and the prevailing circumstances so that it takes appropriate decisions.

Effects of Dissatisfaction in Romantic Relationships.

Animals are created with inborn energy to create their offspring; and they release this energy by practicing sexual intercourse. If this energy is not released or utilized as it was intended, it can be lost in other biological or psychological forms, some of these forms may be harmful to the animal itself.

Authors Rosenhan & Seligman, in their book titled Abnormal Psychology, published in 1995, page 472, give an account which tends to imply that dissatisfaction in matters related to romantic relationships (sexual intercourse) can lead to symptoms which are not directly related to sex. Examples of these symptoms include morbidity, perversion, etc.

Let me ask you this question: How does a human being deal with their need for sex? Or let me put it in this way: What is the relationship between human intelligence and their feelings for sex? In order to make you understand me let me use an example of hunger: How does the human mind operates to deal with feelings of hunger?

If you have also asked yourself these questions you might have realized that the only way to deal with experience of hunger is to satisfy what it insists. Otherwise you will be buried within a short time. Hunger cannot be resisted by intelligence; perhaps, what intelligence can do is to mediate the experience of hunger so that it is satisfied at appropriate time, place and manner.

The same way for sex, what intelligence can do is to mediate it so that it is satisfied in a humanly and determined way. When the sexual urge gets into bodies of animals, it uses its influence to suppress mental strength so that they become reckless disciples of sex (Soble, et al, 1995; *Internet Encyclopedia of Philosophy*).

Due to the influence which accompanies sexual intercourse, sometimes it is regarded as conjugal right, especially for those who are in marriages. One of couples who is not satisfied with the way they acquire this right may sue their spouse and claim for it.

Do You Have a Cruel Partner? Find it Why and How to Deal with Them.

For people who are in relationships, conflicts might be inevitable; this may be due to human nature, or various circumstances encountered. It is important for couples to learn how they would avoid or minimize chances of getting into conflict between themselves. In order to know how to avoid conflicts, they need first to know signs which can bring them into conflicts.

People who are in relationships should know that they are watched by others; for instance their children. If they have children, their conflicts can bring bad impressions to the children and lower their reputation. Therefore, parents (couples) who are in a conflict should deal with it in a way that their children do not see or know it.

Authors Seligman & Rosenhan, in their book titled Abnormal Psychology, 3rd edition, page 483 & 486; and other authors Heit & Meeks, in their book titled Sexuality and Character Education, published in 2001, page 49, write that there are people who gain sexual arousal when they cause pain to others. In psychology this behavior, which is a problem, is known as *sadism*.

In romantic relationships, one spouse may be treating the other in a painful way, and this may feel good to them. If the victim of this treatment is affected undesirably, and they may want to stop it, it is important that they should first try to know its source. The best way to know the source is for couples to talk openly. Remember that when they are in a relationship, couples live as relatives, friends, neighbors, or any name you may call intimate people; so in some situations, they should put this reality into consideration.

Furthermore, life has got a lot of experiences, some of which induce grudge, resentment in people. It happens sometimes when humans experience resentment, they may want to direct it to others, especially those close to them. In psychology, this tendency is called Displacement, as it is explained by author Richard Gross in his book titled Psychology; The Science of Mind and Behavior, 5th edition, page 498, published in 2009.

Another author known as Richard H. Cox, from the University of Kansas State-USA, in his book titled Sports Psychology; Concepts and Applications, page 220-221, published in 1985, shows a statement which imply that people who are frustrated tend to look for relief in different ways (See Frustration-aggression theory); they may want to get relief of their frustrations from other people or objects.

For readers who like to watch football, you might have seen a player who misses to score a goal, or hears a referee's whistle while they are about to score a goal, they throw their hands in air violently. It is because they have been thwarted to accomplish something they believed was almost done. In psychology this is what is called frustration.

Richard H. Cox continues stating that "Overt aggression acts as a catharsis for further aggression; that is pent-up emotions can be purged or discharged by expressing one's feelings through aggression, hostile aggression results in feelings of guilt, these feelings of guilt are expected to cause a decrease in further aggression." (See page 222 and 228).

I can paraphrase his above statement that when a person shows anger, it acts as a relief for them stop further anger, because when they show their anger, there is possibility that they will finally feel guilt; and these guilty feelings cause a decrease in their anger.

For a spouse who is in a relationship with a person with these behaviors, what they can do is to help the spouse decrease their anger by only staying quiet and listening to them, if it is not necessary to respond instantly. If it is necessary to respond instantly, they should first show they support and accept the anger, even if it is against them. In this way it will be easy to turn the feelings from anger into pity within a short time, and therefore be able to return the conversations to normal.

End.

References

Buss, D.& Larsen, R. (2005). *Personality Psychology; Domains of Knowledge About Human Nature*, 2nd Edn, Mc Graw Hill, New York.

Cox, R. (1985). *Sports Psychology; Concepts and Applications*, Wm. C. Brown Publishers, Iowa.

Gökdağ, R., 2015. *Love and Jealousy in Woman-Man Communication*, Online Journal of Communication and Media Technologies, Anadolu University-Turkey.

Gross, R. (2009). *Psychology; The Science of Mind and Behavior*, 5th Edn, Holder Anord Publishers.

Heit, P.& Meeks, L. (2001). *Sexuality and Character Education*, Mc Graw-Hill Companies, New York.

Internet Encyclopedia of Philosophy: *Philosophy of Sexuality*, http://www.iep.utm.edu/sexualit/ (04:14 p.m, Tuesday, May 12, 2015,EAGT).

Luciano, D. S., Sherman, J. H., Vander, A. J., (1985). *Human Physiology*: *The Mechanism of Body Function*, 4th Edn, McGraw-Hill, New York.

Kapicka, C. et al., (1998). *Biology: The Dynamics of Life*, McGraw Hill, New York.

Pecorino, P. A., (2000). *An Introduction to Philisophy; Socrates Legacy*, https://www.qcc.cuny.edu/socialsciences/ppecorino/intro_text/Chapter%202%20GREEKS/Socrates_Legacy.htm. Imesomwa mtandaoni tarehe 17th November, 2022.

Pennington, D.C., (1999). *Social Psychology*, Oxford University, New York.

Pigliucci, M., (2011). *Ignorance Today*; An Article on Aljazeera, https://www.aljazeera.com/opinions/2011/7/18/ignorance-today.

Rosenhan, D. & Seligman M. (1995). *Abnormal Psychology*, 3rd Edn, Norton and Company, New York.

Soble, A. et al. (2002). *The Philosophy of Sex; Contemporary Readings*, 4th Edn, Rowans & Littlefield Publishers, Inc. USA. http://www.webmd.com/sex-relationships/guide/why-people-have-sex (12:24 p.m, Tuesday, May 12, 2015,EAGT).